URBAN GARDENING AND FARMING FOR TEENS™

JARRING AND CANNING

MAKE YOUR OWN JAMS, JELLIES, PICKLES, AND MORE

BRIDGET HEOS

ROSEN
PUBLISHING®

New York

Published in 2014 by The Rosen Publishing Group, Inc.
29 East 21st Street, New York, NY 10010

First Edition

Library of Congress Cataloging-in-Publication Data

Heos, Bridget.
Jarring and canning: make your own jams, jellies, pickles, and more/
Bridget Heos.—1st ed.
        p. cm.—(Urban gardening and farming for teens)
ISBN 978-1-4777-1780-6 (library binding)
1. Canning and preserving. I. Title. II. Series: Urban gardening and farming
for teens.
TX603.H485 2014
664'.0282—dc23

2013022709

Manufactured in the United States of America

CPSIA Compliance Information: Batch #W14YA: For further information, contact Rosen Publishing, New York, New York, at 1-800-237-9932.

Contents

Introduction

The teenagers of BoysGrow, an urban farming group in Kansas City, Missouri, had too much of a good thing: vegetables. And they had no refrigerated storage. After driving around to local restaurants and selling the produce to chefs, they still had leftovers. So they made salsa and sold that, too.

Canned or jarred vegetables, whether plain or mixed as a condiment like salsa, last for up to a year without being refrigerated. That means teens who grow fruit or vegetables can stretch out their harvest season longer. Some teens, like those in BoysGrow, sell their jarred products. The group also made ketchup with their summer tomato harvest. Other teens keep them for their families so that they won't have to buy fruits and vegetables in the winter.

Canning and jarring is part of the urban farming and gardening movement sweeping America. Teens are growing vegetables on vacant land in and around cities in order to spend time outside, learn valuable work skills, and harvest food for their communities. John Gordon Jr. founded BoysGrow, which pays the teens for their work on the urban farm. More than just a job, the farming is meaningful work that requires creative thinking and a good work ethic. "They're going to be connected to something that they like that they get paid for and want to see

A young girl weeds a garden that provides food for a soup kitchen in Detroit, Michigan. Many young people like her have joined the urban farming movement.

grow," Gordon told the *Kansas City Star*. "To me that's the best thing we can do."

Jarring and canning was once a common practice in households that grew fruits and vegetables. Many high schools even offered lessons in canning through home economics classes. Today, people may be more likely to buy produce at the grocery store. But home canned fruits and vegetables have the garden freshness that you can't get in a store, plus they're economical. So some urban gardeners are returning to the practice of preserving. If you're interested in joining them, you can learn all about it here.

CHAPTER ONE

JOINING THE FRESH FOOD MOVEMENT

Canning is a way of preserving food by killing bacteria with heat and then creating an airtight seal to prevent the growth of new bacteria. It was created by French chef Nicolas Appert in the late 1700s. (Other scientists also contributed to food preservation, including Louis Pasteur, who discovered that air needed to be removed so that bacteria wouldn't grow.) At the time, many people still grew fresh food on their own land, however small the space. But soldiers and sailors relied on stored food. During the Napoleonic Wars, many soldiers were dying of malnutrition and botulism (sickness from eating spoiled food). Appert's preserved foods were introduced to the troops, saving lives. Preserved fruits and vegetables also prevented scurvy in sailors, a sickness caused by lack of vitamin C.

Appert opened a factory to preserve food in jars. Other factories followed suit, but they used cans to preserve their goods instead. In the mid-1800s, Mason jars made home canning convenient. By then, many people had moved from rural to urban areas to find work during the Industrial Revolution. Tenement

Historically, people have enjoyed the taste of fresh fruit and vegetables throughout the year by canning produce from their gardens. In this 1950 photo, a woman illustrates her stocked pantry.

housing offered little space or sunlight, so city-dwellers had to buy, rather than grow, their own food. But for those who still had a bit of land, "putting up" jars for the winter became a yearly tradition. During World War II, many people raised victory gardens and preserved their food in jars to cope with government food rations. The popularity of home canning died out afterward. But recently, jarring has grown in popularity as part of the urban gardening movement.

Urban farms or gardens are plots of fertile land in the city. Growers take advantage of small spaces, such as rooftops, vacant lots, and yards. Teens are turning to urban gardening in order to get outside, learn agricultural skills, grow healthy food, and build communities. They are also combating problems such as food deserts, factory farms, and a sedentary lifestyle.

WHY JOIN THE URBAN GARDEN MOVEMENT?

According to the *Week*, 23.5 million Americans live in a food desert, defined as an area where at least 20 percent of the people live under the poverty line, and 33 percent live a mile (1.6 kilometers) away from a supermarket (or 10 miles [16 km] away in rural areas). This can lead residents to rely on fast food and convenience store items, as opposed to healthy choices like fruit and vegetables. Eating fruits and vegetables prevents diseases and promotes good health. But according to a January 28, 2007, article in *Science Daily*, teens aren't eating nearly enough. Girls' fruit and vegetable intake drops, on average, from four to three servings from junior high to high school, well below the recommended seven servings per day. Boys are eating even less. Their fruit and vegetable servings drop from 2 ½ to 1 ½ from junior high to high school, at a

Teens across America are getting fewer than their recommended daily servings of fruits and vegetables. Those who live in food deserts have limited access to fresh produce.

time when they should be eating nine servings per day. Authors of the study theorized that the lack of tasty fruit and vegetable choices, along with fewer family dinners each week, explained the unhealthy trend. Growing fruit and vegetables provides teens with nutritious food regardless of their neighborhood resources. And homegrown fruit and vegetables—even in jars—tend to taste better than store-bought varieties.

Urban gardens are not only helpful to teens and their families but to the whole neighborhood, as they cut down on urban blight (which in turn cuts down on crime). When people convert vacant or unused land to garden space, they become stewards of that land. Studies have shown that rundown property attracts crime, whereas cared-for property does the opposite. Also, when people are outside tending gardens, they talk to each other and keep an eye on things. This builds friendship and community.

Another reason teens are joining the urban gardening movement is to get outdoors. The American Academy of Pediatrics recommends that kids and teens spend an hour outside each day for optimal physical and mental health. But in reality, the Nature Conservancy reports, only 6 percent of children play outside on their own on a typical day. On the other hand, children average more than seven hours a day on entertainment media—practically all of their free time after school. With 80 percent of the U.S. population living in urban areas, according to the *San Francisco Chronicle*, it's not surprising that teens have lost touch with the natural world. The proportion of children ages nine to twelve who spent time hiking, fishing, walking, playing on the beach, or gardening declined 50 percent between 1997 and 2003. Urban gardening gets teens back in touch with the natural world and teaches them to rely on nature for food. As with any skill, once they master one aspect of urban gardening, other skills start to make sense. For instance, you may start by raising vegetables for your family. Soon you may decide, like the BoysGrow group, to make and sell salsa and ketchup. Now you have a business, too.

Some teens have begun raising food out of concern for the modern industrial food system. The modern food industry relies on the transportation of produce from hundreds of miles away, which leads to carbon emissions that contribute to global warming. Large-scale fertilization of crops pollutes waterways and contributes to global warming. Raising your own food cuts down

When you grow your own vegetables, you can choose from a wider variety than is available at the grocery store. For instance, tomatoes can be orange, purple, striped, and more.

on carbon emissions and allows you to fertilize responsibly. At home, you can also raise a wider variety of fruits and vegetables. For instance, did you know that tomatoes can be yellow, greenish, and purplish? Produce has become so homogenized that many consumers don't know what they're missing. Visit a garden store and you'll soon discover what nature has to offer. Finally, homegrown fruit and vegetables taste better, since you can focus on quality over quantity. You can feed your soil the nutrients it needs, let the fruit ripen in the sun, and eat it while it is still warm and fresh—or fresh from the jar.

Unlike purchased canned goods, home-canned foods retain the freshness of the garden. You can use your imagination to

BEGINNER JAM

Strawberry freezer jam requires minimal cooking, and the jars do not have to be boiled. Instead, they are stored in the freezer until ready to eat. This is a good jam to ease into home canning, as it requires very few supplies.

SUPPLIES:
Mixing bowl
Saucepan
5 1-cup plastic containers
with lids

INGREDIENTS:
1 quart strawberries
4 cups sugar
¾ cups water
1 package Sure-Jell

INSTRUCTIONS:
1. Remove stems from strawberries and crush them with a potato masher or fork. Put two cups in the mixing bowl.
2. Stir sugar into crushed strawberries and let stand for ten minutes, stirring occasionally.
3. In the saucepan over high heat, mix water and pectin and bring to a boil for one minute, stirring constantly. Pour this over the fruit mixture and stir for three minutes. All of the sugar should be dissolved.
4. Pour the mixture into the five plastic containers, leaving .5 inch (1.3 centimeters) at the top. Cover with lids, and let stand for twenty-four hours.
5. Refrigerate the containers you will eat in three weeks. Freeze the rest for up to a year. Thaw before eating.

(From KraftRecipes.com)

create tasty flavors that you can't find in the store. (For instance, like tomatoes, ketchup has been homogenized. How about making grape ketchup instead?) Canning has the reputation for being a lot of work, but preserving a small amount of produce is really no different than a day of baking, and the results last longer. Plan to start small. The first time you jar, don't feel like you need to prepare for the end of the world or make enough for the whole neighborhood. That may lead to frustration, and your first time canning will also be your last. Just pick one or two things that you've grown in your garden and try to fill five to ten jars. Be sure to educate yourself so that you feel confident as you begin the day. You can:

- Read sources like this one.
- Join groups like 4-H. 4-H is a youth organization that includes gardening and food preservation programs. Though traditionally associated with rural areas, 4-H is growing in cities.
- Take a class from a college, gardening group, farmer's market, or nature center.
- Ask an older relative or neighbor who grew up canning for advice.
- Ask your school to offer a class on canning, particularly if you already have a school garden.

(Note: The terms "canning" and "jarring" are used interchangeably. The term "canning" is more common. However, for most home operations, jars are used. Whether referring to the process as jarring or canning, the instructions and recipes given here are for putting food in jars.)

CHAPTER TWO

GETTING STARTED

So are you ready to join the home canning movement? Before you start, decide what you'd like to accomplish. Do you hope to set aside food for your family to eat in the winter? Make gifts for family and friends? Sell your items? If you plan to sell your products, whom will you sell to? It doesn't take much money to get started canning. Many of the supplies are probably already in your kitchen. You can save money by buying other items at garage sales. You'll need:

- A stovetop.
- Pots. You'll need a six- to ten-quart pot for cooking the items you plan to can and a small saucepan for simmering lids.
- Canning pot and rack. You'll need a large pot, wide enough to hold the rack and deep enough to cover jars by an inch (2.5 cm) and allow the water to boil. You can buy a canning rack or use a cake cooling rack. You can also combine these two items by buying a canner, which is a pot and rack specifically for canning.

Jars are lifted in and out of pots with a metal rack, which comes with a canner. This woman is sterilizing the jars prior to filling them.

- Jars. Buy jars made specifically for canning, such as Ball or Kerr brands. These can withstand heat and seal air-tight, both essential for safely preparing and storing your jars. For fruits and vegetables, you'll generally use pint or quart jars. (There are two pints in a quart.) For jellies and jams, you may use a half-pint. You'll need regular-mouth jars for jams and jellies, and wide-mouth jars for fruits and vegetables. The glass jars can be reused, but you'll always need to buy new flat sealing lids.

- Other canning supplies. A jar lifter, wide-mouthed funnel, candy thermometer, fine mesh strainer, and timer will come in handy.

- Miscellaneous. You'll need measuring cups and spoons, knives, ladles, slotted spoons, large bowls, a colander, and dish towels.

- Common ingredients. These include sugar, vinegar, herbs, pectin (for jams and jellies), lemon juice, and salt.

HOW MUCH WILL THIS COST?

You probably already have basic kitchen supplies, like pots, spoons, and measuring cups. Here are approximate prices of items specifically for jarring:

Jars $2–$3 each
Large canner with rack $20
Jar lifter $6
Thermometer $6
Funnel $3
Sugar $3/5 pound bag
Vinegar $3/gallon
Pectin $7/to make 22 half-pints of jam

And of course, you'll need fresh produce. Good vegetables, fruits, and herbs to grow for jarring include cucumbers and dill for pickles, strawberries for jam and syrup, berries, apples, cherries, peaches, and tomatoes. You may not be able to grow all these things, especially apples, cherries, and peaches, which grow on trees. But you could visit an orchard or farmer's market, or trade with a neighbor.

SAFETY AND THE BASICS

It's important to consider the safety of jarring food. Eating food that has spoiled because it wasn't jarred correctly can result in the disease botulism. Be sure to follow directions and seal jars properly. Check seals before storing. Press on the lid; it should not move or make a noise. Nobody is perfect, so it's important to

Fruits that are high in acid can be canned through water bath canning. Acid like lemon juice can also be added to low-acid fruits like tomatoes during the canning process.

be wary. When you open the jar to eat the contents, you should hear a pop. If the food looks or smells funny, throw it away. Don't taste it to see if it's gone bad.

The point of jarring is to stop bacterial growth. Acidic foods, like many fruits, are less prone to bacterial growth. Acid, such as vinegar or lemon juice, can be added to other items, like cucumbers and tomatoes, to stop bacterial growth. Otherwise, low-in-acid fruits, vegetables, and meats must be processed at high heat because they are more prone to bacteria. High heat is achieved through a pressure canner (described later). Other canning is called water bath canning, hot water bath canning, or boiling water bath canning. No matter what it is called, it requires boiling the jars, as that kills the bacteria.

THE BASICS OF WATER BATH CANNING

First, go through your recipe and determine what supplies you'll need. Make sure your jars have no chips or cracks. Next you'll boil the jars, which sterilizes and heats them, preventing cracking later. Put the jars on the rack and the rack in the canning pot. Fill the pot with water, letting the jars fill, too. Bring the water to a boil. In the meantime, put the lids in a small saucepan, fill it with water, and bring to a simmer. Now make your recipe.

With jar tongs, remove the jars from the boiling water and place them open-side-up on a towel. Remove the lids from the simmering water with tongs and place them on the towel, too. Using the wide-mouthed funnel, fill the jars with the recipe, leaving either .25 inch (0.6 cm) or .5 inch (1.3 cm) at the top. (The recipe will indicate if one-half inch is needed. Otherwise, leave one-fourth inch.) Place the flat lid on the jar. With a hot,

Kept in a cool, dry place, canned fruits and vegetables should last a year. Here, you see the wide variety of produce that can be canned.

wet washcloth, wipe off any spills around the lid. Then screw on the band with your fingertips (so that it is not too tight to open later).

Lower the filled jars into the boiling water in the canning pot, scooping out water to make more room if needed. Once the water comes back to a boil, start your timer. Boiling the filled cans is called "processing." The processing time varies by recipe. When the timer goes off, remove the jars. Place them on a towel to cool. You will hear popping from the seals forming on the lids. Let them cool for a full day. Now remove the ring. This will NOT break the seal. To test the seal, lift the jar a couple inches by the flat lid. It should hold. If it doesn't, that means the seal is bad. Store the jar in the refrigerator and eat the contents within two weeks. If the seal is good, store it without the ring or with the ring re-screwed on loosely. Kept in a cool, dry place, your preserved jars should last a year. However, if stored in the open, or near a heat source, they may last only a few months. Those are the basics of jarring. For specifics on jarring fruits, jams, vegetables, and pickled foods, read on.

CHAPTER THREE

FRUITS IN SYRUP AND FRUIT SYRUP

Jarred fruit works as a side dish or dessert. You can also stir it into oatmeal or yogurt, or bake it in a dessert. In the store, you've probably seen fruit described as being canned in light syrup or heavy syrup. That describes the sugar content. If you prefer light syrup, use two cups of sugar for every four cups of water. For medium syrup, add three cups of sugar to four cups of water. And for heavy syrup, use four and three-quarters cups of sugar for four cups of water. Why is naturally sweet fruit packed in syrup at all? It helps the fruit retain its flavor, shape, and color. In some cases, however, you can pack the fruit in water or juice instead.

Packing is the process of filling jars. There is hot packing, and there is cold, or raw, packing. With hot packing, you cook the fruit in the syrup or other liquid, and then pour it into the jars. With cold packing, you put the raw fruit in the jars, cook the hot liquid, and pour the liquid over the raw fruit. Either way,

Peaches are a favorite canned fruit. Freestone peach pits pull away from the fruit more easily during preparation, making them a better choice for canning.

you then boil, or process, the sealed jars. You must boil the full jars right away. Jars that have cooled and are then reheated can break. Some fruits need to be hot packed or cold packed, but others can be packed either way.

SPECIFICS ON MAKING JARRED FRUIT

The following are directions for making popular jarred fruit. Remember, you'll follow the basics described earlier, beginning with boiling your jars and simmering your lids.

Peaches. Have you ever noticed that some peach pits pop right out of the fruit, whereas others are immovable? That's because there are two types of peaches: freestone, in which the pits pull away from the fruit easily, and clingstone, in which the pits cling to the fruit. Freestone peaches are better for canning. You'll need about two and a half pounds of peaches per quart jar. Boil your peaches for a minute, and then plunge them in cold water. Now peel. Cut each peach in half and remove the pit. Next, plunge the peaches in a gallon of water, two tablespoons of salt, and two tablespoons of vinegar. Drain. Boil the peaches in medium syrup just long enough to heat. Fill the jars with the peaches and syrup, and seal the jars. Process (boil) pint jars for fifteen minutes, or quart jars for twenty minutes.

Pears. About two and a half pounds of pears can also fit in a quart jar. Peel, cut in half, and remove the cores. Prepare the same as peaches (skipping the hot peeling step).

Pineapple. About three pounds of pineapples per quart jar are needed. Pare and slice the pineapples into rings or chunks. Simmer in light syrup until tender. Pour the pineapple and syrup in jars, leaving one-half inch at the top. Seal and boil for fifteen minutes for a pint, or twenty minutes for a quart.

Apples. About two and three-quarters pounds of apples are needed per quart. Peel, core, and cut in quarters. Cook in syrup for two to four minutes (until tender). Fill jars with apples and syrup. Seal and boil for fifteen minutes for pints, twenty minutes for quarts.

Berries. About one and three-quarters pounds of berries fill a quart jar. You can use raspberries, blackberries, boysenberries, and more. It's not recommended to jar strawberries. Save those for jam! For berries it's best to raw pack the jars. Fill the jars

Berries make delicious jams and syrups, but they can also be canned whole (with the exception of strawberries). It's best not to cook berries prior to canning.

with raw fruit. Boil syrup (light, medium, or heavy) and pour it over the fruit to cover. Seal and boil for fifteen minutes for pint or quart jars. You can also pour boiling juice or water over the raw fruit instead of syrup.

HOW MANY FRUITS AND VEGETABLES DO I NEED TO EAT?

Teenage boys need nine servings of fruit or vegetables, and teenage girls seven. If that seems like a lot, keep in mind that you can eat more than one serving at a time. For instance, a main course salad would typically have three cups of lettuce (three servings) and a smoothie can contain two or three servings of fruit. Here are some examples of single servings:

6 ounces of fruit juice
1 cup salad or other leafy vegetables
½ cup other raw vegetables
½ cup cooked vegetables
½ cup berries or chopped fruit
¼ cup dried fruit
1 medium piece of fruit

To add more servings to your diet, top ice cream, yogurt, pancakes, and waffles with your jarred fruit, stir salsa into your eggs, add canned tomatoes to cheese sauce, and top your sandwiches with homemade pickles.

Cherries. About two and a half pounds of cherries fill a quart jar. Pit the cherries. Fill the jars with a half cup of hot water, juice, or syrup. Add cherries, leaving .5 inch (1.3 cm) at the top. Add hot water, juice, or syrup to .5 inch from the top. Boil pints or quarts for twenty-five minutes.

Grapefruit. You'll need about two pounds of grapefruit per quart jar. Peel the grapefruit, separate the segments, and remove the skin from each segment. Put the segments in the jar, and cover with hot syrup. Boil pints for twenty minutes, and quarts for twenty-five minutes.

(Fruit canning directions from the University of Georgia Cooperative Extension and *Canning & Preserving* by Linda Ferrari.)

Strawberry syrup. Fruit syrups can be poured over ice cream or pancakes, stirred into oatmeal, or added to sparkling water to make homemade soft drinks. Boil four half-pint jars and simmer the lids. Boil two pints of hulled and chopped strawberries with three cups of water for fifteen minutes. Strain the strawberries and liquid over a sieve. Throw away the solids. Return the juice to the pot and add two cups of sugar. Bring to a boil. Skim the foam off the top. Pour the syrup into jars, leaving .5 inch (1.3 cm) at the top. Seal and boil for ten minutes. (From *Food in Jars* by Marisa McClellan.)

CHAPTER FOUR

JAMS, JELLIES, BUTTERS, PRESERVES, MARMALADES, AND MORE

Nothing starts the day like warm toast spread with butter and jam. Or jelly. Or preserves. Or marmalade. Or, wait a second, what's the difference?

Jam is a thick spread made from fruit, sugar, and pectin. It's the easiest of the above to make. Jelly is a clear but thick spread made from fruit juice, sugar, pectin, and acid. (In Great Britain, jelly is a dessert similar to Jell-O, sometimes served with ice cream on birthdays.) Fruit butter is slow-cooked fruit and sugar. Preserves are jellies with chunks of fruit. Marmalade is a spread made from citrus fruit.

Most people start out making jam. For jam, you'll need fruit, sugar, and pectin. Pectin is a substance that occurs naturally in fruit. It's what causes jams and jellies to gel. In the old days, people cooked their jams and jellies long enough for the fruits' naturally occurring pectin to react. Today, most people add pectin separately, which reduces the cooking time. Recipes may call for liquid or powdered pectin. Freezer jam requires instant pectin, whereas traditional jams and jellies require regular pectin.

Strawberry jam is a thick spread made from fruit, sugar, and pectin. It differs from strawberry jelly, which is made with juice and is translucent.

To make raspberry jam, prepare eight half-pint jars. In an eight- to ten-quart pot, crush eight cups of raspberries using a potato masher or fork. Stir in pectin. Bring to a boil, stirring constantly. Add seven cups of sugar. Bring to a boil, stirring. Boil for a minute. Remove from heat. Skim the foam off the top. Ladle into jars and seal. Boil in the canner for five minutes. Remove and cool. (From *Can It!* by Better Homes & Gardens.)

BEYOND TOAST: JAM ALL DAY LONG

Besides slathering jam, jelly, marmalade, or apple butter on toast, you can:

FOR BREAKFAST:

Slather it on pancakes or waffles.

Add it to plain yogurt or oatmeal.

Make homemade Pop Tarts: Cut uncooked pie crust into equal rectangles. Spread jam onto one rectangle. Top with another rectangle. Press around the edges with a fork. Prick the top with holes. Freeze for thirty minutes. Bake at 375 degrees F (190 degrees C) for thirty to thirty-five minutes.

FOR LUNCH:

Make French toast sandwiches. Arrange ham or turkey and Swiss between two slices of bread. Whisk two eggs and a little milk. Melt one tablespoon butter in a pan over medium heat. Dip one side of the sandwich bread into the egg mixture. Cook the sandwich in the pan, egg side down. Spoon egg mixture onto the slice of bread facing up. Flip the sandwich and cook the other side. Remove from pan. Sprinkle with powdered sugar and serve with hot jam.

FOR A SNACK:

Slather over cream cheese or brie for a cracker spread.

Make sandwich cookies with vanilla wafers.

FOR DINNER:

Warm and serve over pork, beef, or chicken.

Mix with vinegar and oil for a sweet salad dressing.

FOR DESSERT:

Make a trifle (layered dessert) with angel food cake, jam or jelly, fruit, pudding, and whipped cream.

Warm jam and pour over ice cream.

If you haven't tried making homemade jelly, Concord grape is a good place to start. Jelly is a two-step process that involves making juice first. To speed the process, you can buy unsweetened juice instead. Here is the recipe for a small batch: Place a saucer or small plate in the freezer. Prepare four half-pint jars. Whisk three cups sugar and one 1.75-ounce packet powdered pectin. In a large pot, combine four cups Concord grape juice and the pectin and sugar mixture. Bring to a boil and cook for fifteen to twenty-five minutes (until the pot reaches 220 degrees F [104 degrees C]). Test the jelly's readiness with the saucer test: take the saucer out of the freezer and spoon a little jelly onto it. Freeze for two to three minutes. It should firm up. If the jelly remains syrupy, cook it for five more minutes. When it passes the saucer test, pour it into the jars and boil them for ten minutes. (From FoodinJars.com.)

Concord grapes are a candylike variety of grape that can be used for making grape juice. But more important, they are used for making Concord grape jelly.

To make your own grape juice, stem and wash four pounds of Concord grapes. Place in a saucepan and smash with a potato masher. Bring the grapes and juice to a boil over low heat. Continue mashing. When it comes to a boil, remove from heat. Let cool a few minutes. Strain in a sieve, smashing the grapes to get more juice. Throw away the solids and save the juice. (From SpadeSpatula.com.)

If you grow watermelons, you probably have plenty during the summer. Watermelon doesn't do well as jarred fruit, but you can make watermelon jelly. Prepare five half-pint jars. Remove seeds and puree watermelon in a blender to make six cups. Separately, whisk together five cups of sugar with one 1.75-ounce packet of pectin. Now combine the sugar mixture, watermelon, and six tablespoons of lemon juice in a pot. Boil until the jelly reaches 220 degrees F (104 degrees C). Do the saucer test. Pour into jars and boil for ten minutes. (From FoodinJars.com.)

If you live in a warm climate, you may be lucky enough to have an orange or lemon tree. Interestingly, orange marmalade is most popular in Great Britain and former British colonies. Britain isn't known for its orange trees, so what gives? Marmalade dates to ancient Greece, but for centuries, quince was the fruit used. Quince trees grew in Great Britain, and quince marmalade was popular there. Then, in Scotland, Seville oranges began being imported from Spain. Orange replaced quince as the marmalade fruit of choice. British people fell in love with orange marmalade. It is mentioned in works ranging from *Alice in Wonderland* by Lewis Carroll to "Lucy in the Sky with Diamonds" by the Beatles. British colonies also adapted the tradition, substituting local fruits, such as grapefruit for the oranges. America is the only former colony not particularly in love with orange marmalade, perhaps because citrus fruit wasn't readily available in the early colonies.

Here is a recipe for lemon marmalade: Rinse twelve Meyer lemons (sweet lemons) and pat them dry. Cut the lemons in half and juice them, removing the seeds. Scrape the remaining fruit from the peels. Slice the peels one-eighth inch (0.3 cm) thick. Boil the strips for one minute. Drain and rinse in cold water. Repeat this step twice. The final time, do not rinse the peels. In the dry saucepan, add the peels, juice, and three cups of sugar. Simmer for thirty minutes, skimming foam from the top. Pour into five prepared half-pint jars, leaving .25 inch (0.6 cm) at the top. Boil for fifteen minutes and let set for two days. (From *Food & Wine.*)

Apple butter, on the other hand, is as American as apple pie and *tastes* like apple pie. This is an easy recipe for refrigerator apple butter, which you can enjoy on toast or crackers. To make this fall treat, peel and core four apples and chop into equal-size pieces. Add the apples to a large pot, along with one-half cup brown sugar, two tablespoons cider or water, and cinnamon. Cover the pot and cook on low for twenty minutes. Remove the lid, raise heat to medium, and cook for ten more minutes. Add three tablespoons butter and mash the apples. Store in an airtight container for two weeks in the refrigerator. (From *PBS Food.*)

CHAPTER FIVE

CANNING VEGETABLES

Care must be taken when preserving vegetables. Because they are low in acid, they are more susceptible to bacteria growth. To prevent this, you can add acid in the form of lemon juice or vinegar. You can also process vegetables in a pressure canner, which we'll discuss here. Unlike a regular canner, which can be any large pot with a rack placed inside, a pressure canner is a specific piece of equipment. It has a clamp lid and weight gage, which determines the pressure at which the jars of vegetables cook. A pressure canner raises the temperature at which water boils from 212 degrees F (100 degrees C) to up to 250 degrees F (121 degrees C). The high heat, combined with the pressure, kills the bacteria. On the low end, they cost $80. (A pressure canner is not the same as a pressure cooker. Though similar in concept, a pressure cooker will not adequately process canned vegetables.)

GO BACK TO YOUR ROOTS WITH A ROOT CELLAR

Before refrigeration, root cellars were a common way to store vegetables raised on the farm. Some people still choose this method because refrigerated storage is expensive, and the same coolness can be achieved underground. Traditionally, root cellars were dirt floor basements that sometimes doubled as storm cellars in case of a tornado. But you can also use crawl spaces under your house, or make a root cellar by burying a barrel. The temperature needs to be 32–40 degrees F (0–4.4 degrees C) for most vegetables, and humidity around 90 percent. Ventilation is necessary. Store vegetables and fruits separately, as gases from the fruit will cause vegetables to sprout. Under the right conditions, standard root vegetables like potatoes and carrots will last four to six months underground. For more information, consult your college extension.

Alison Gannet retrieves jars from her root cellar. She lives on a 75-acre (4,047 square meters) organic farm, where she grows almost all of the food she eats throughout the year.

If you know others who want to can vegetables, you might consider sharing a pressure canner. In this case, it's best to use a new pressure canner, or one that you know was well taken care of. That way, it will work properly. In the past, pressure canners occasionally blew up. But new models are safe as long as you follow directions and continuously monitor the pressure gage. Having access to a pressure canner allows you to jar what might be the bulk of your garden produce: corn, green beans, carrots, peppers, pumpkin, and other vegetables. You can also can meat using a pressure canner, although that is not covered here.

THE BASICS OF CANNING VEGETABLES

You begin canning vegetables in the same manner that you can fruit, by boiling the empty jars and simmering the lids. This should be done in ordinary pots. Next, vegetables are typically boiled in salt water and packed in jars. The jars are placed in the pressure canner. Then the pressure canner is clamped shut and heated on the stove over high heat. It boils, and steam vents out through a hole in the lid. After ten minutes, you adjust the pressure as directed (usually to ten pounds) and cook for the recommended time. Here are directions for jarring some common vegetables:

To can corn, prepare jars. Shuck the corn, cut the raw kernels from the cob, and place them in a pot. (Four and a half pounds of corn in the husk will result in one quart of canned corn.) Cover with salt water (one tablespoon of salt per quart of water). Heat to boiling. Pour into jars and seal. Cook at ten pounds pressure for fifty-five minutes for pints, or seventy minutes for quart jars.

Corn on the cob can be shucked and canned, but because it is low in acid, it must be processed in a pressure canner to kill bacteria.

For green beans, snip the ends and chop into one-inch pieces. (You'll need an average of two pounds per quart.) Boil for two to five minutes and pack into jars. Add one-half teaspoon salt for a pint, or one teaspoon for a quart. Cover to ¾ an inch (1.9 cm) from the top with the boiling liquid. Seal. Cook at ten pounds pressure for twenty minutes for pints or twenty-five minutes for quarts.

For pumpkin, remove the pulp and skin the outside. Cut the flesh into one-inch cubes. (You'll need two and a quarter pounds per quart.) The pumpkin cubes should be boiled and immediately packed to .5 inch (1.3 cm) of the top of the jar. One-half teaspoon of salt should be added to pints, and one teaspoon to quarts. Liquid should cover the pumpkins. Once the jars are sealed, they should be cooked in the pressure canner for fifty-five minutes for pints, or ninety minutes for quarts.

Carrots (two and a half pounds per quart) should be cold-packed. After peeling and slicing, pack the carrots to 1 inch (2.5

cm) of the top of the jar. One teaspoon of salt should be added to pint or quart jars. Then add boiling water to three-fourths the tops of the jars. Boil in the pressure canner for thirty minutes for pints or quarts. (Vegetable canning instructions from *Canning and Preserving* by Linda Ferrari.)

Another way to preserve fresh vegetables is to freeze them. Before being frozen, some vegetables must be blanched, or steamed but not fully cooked. This stops the enzymes that cause food to decay even in freezing temperatures. After steaming, they are plunged in cold water to stop further cooking. Then they must be fully drained and stored in freezer-safe containers, such as plastic tubs or freezer bags. Common frozen vegetables that

If you don't want to invest in a pressure canner, you can freeze vegetables instead. For instance, homegrown potatoes can easily be transformed into frozen hash browns or French fries.

need to be blanched include asparagus, green beans, broccoli, cauliflower, Brussels sprouts, okra, peas, and squash. Onions, tomatoes, and corn do not need to be blanched. Most frozen vegetables store well for eight months to a year. But tomatoes keep for only about three months, so it's best to check sources like university extensions when you freeze specific vegetables.

To freeze broccoli, first clean it thoroughly, as insects tend to hide in the florets. Soak for thirty minutes in salt water (four teaspoons per gallon), and then rinse. Trim the stalk and chop into pieces. To blanch, steam for six minutes or boil for four minutes. Cool and drain, pack in a freezer safe container, and freeze.

Freezing is a good way to preserve greens like spinach, which are not recommended to be canned at home. Choose young leaves. Wash and remove stems and any bad parts. Blanche for two and a half minutes, drain, and freeze. For hardier greens, like kale and collards, blanch for four minutes, drain, and freeze.

If you grow potatoes, you can make your own frozen hash browns or French fries. For hash browns, you'll almost fully cook the potatoes and peel them. Then shred the potatoes and freeze them. French fries require peeling, slicing, and frying in 360-degree F (182 degrees C) oil for four minutes. Drain, cool, and freeze.

CHAPTER SIX

TOMATOES AND TOMATO SAUCES

Of all the store-bought vegetables, tomatoes have perhaps the worst reputation for being mushy and flavorless. These tomatoes are bred for quantity not quality. Year-round tomatoes also tend to be grown in warm climates but poor soil. On the other hand, tomatoes are easy to grow at home, needing only a small plot of warm soil, a little water, and plenty of sunlight. Varieties range from tiny cherry tomatoes to giant, juicy fruits. With six or so plants, you'll have more tomatoes than you know what to do with. That's when you can them—either as is, or as salsa, tomato sauce, or ketchup.

In the old days, tomatoes (technically a fruit) were often as acidic as many other fruits. Today's tomatoes have been bred to be sweeter. So you need to add lemon juice when canning. This is true even of heirloom tomatoes, the acidity of which is unpredictable. For whole peeled tomatoes, you'll want to grow small to medium tomatoes. Paste tomatoes such as Roma are often used for these and other canned tomatoes. You'll need two

Rich soil and vine ripening give homegrown tomatoes their robust flavor. Extra fruit can be canned as peeled whole tomatoes, diced tomatoes, tomato sauce, ketchup, salsa, and more.

and a half to three and a half pounds per quart jar. Don't use overripe or damaged tomatoes, and be sure to pick your tomatoes before the first frost. Start by boiling the tomatoes for one minute until the skins crack. Dip into cold water, peel, and core. Bring the prepared tomatoes to a boil. Pack into prepared quart jars. Cover with the liquid in which they were boiled. Add one teaspoon salt, one teaspoon sugar, and one tablespoon lemon juice per quart jar. Seal and boil for forty-five minutes.

Diced tomatoes are handy for soup, stew, chili, and cheese dips. To can diced tomatoes, peel the tomatoes (according to the previous directions). Then dice the tomatoes in even chunks. Boil the diced tomatoes, fill the prepared jars, and add one teaspoon salt and two tablespoons vinegar or lemon juice per quart. Seal the jars, and boil for forty-five minutes.

Tomato sauce is commonly used for pasta, pizza, Spanish rice, and soup. It can be made from scratch and jarred. To make five quarts, you'll need ten pounds of tomatoes, one minced red pepper, one minced large onion, one and a half tablespoons salt, two teaspoons pepper, a quarter cup lemon juice, and a half cup vinegar. Boil the tomatoes for thirty seconds and peel, core, and quarter them. Cook all ingredients in a saucepan for forty minutes. Then liquefy in the blender. Cook again for thirty minutes. Fill five quart jars, and boil for forty-five minutes. (From *Canning & Preserving* by Linda Ferrari.)

Salsa should be made with paste tomatoes, such as Roma. These are fleshier than slicing varieties and make thicker salsa. If you've made salsa, you may have experimented with ingredients and quantities. That's fine if you plan to eat the salsa right away. But to preserve salsa, you must follow the recipe

It's fine to experiment with salsa when you plan to eat it right away. For canned salsa, however, you must follow the recipe exactly to achieve the desired acidity.

exactly in order to maintain a safe acid level to deter bacterial growth. The only exception is the herbs. For instance, substituting cilantro for oregano won't affect the acidity of the salsa. Here is one basic recipe: combine the following ingredients in a large saucepan—eight quarts peeled, cored, and chopped tomatoes; two crushed cloves garlic; five cups chopped onions; four seeded and chopped jalapenos; four seeded and chopped green chilies; two and a half cups bottled lemon or lime juice; two tablespoons salt; one tablespoon black pepper; one tablespoon sugar; two tablespoons oregano leaves; one teaspoon cumin. Bring to a boil and then reduce heat and simmer for an hour. Pour into prepared pint jars, leaving .5 inch (1.3 cm) at the top. Seal the lids and boil the jars for twenty minutes. (From University of Wisconsin Extension.)

FOR THIS KETCHUP, HOLD THE TOMATOES

Did you know that ketchup doesn't have to be made with tomatoes? Tomatoes have always been a popular ingredient, but in the past, grape, walnut, and fish ketchup were also popular jarred goods in the American pantry. Grape ketchup can be a marinade for meat, a topping for cheese and crackers, or a dip for meatballs or grilled cheese. Here is a recipe:

6 cups seedless red grapes
4 cups apple cider vinegar
6 cups sugar
2 tablespoons cinnamon
2 tablespoons cloves

Prepare eight half-pint jars. Simmer the first three ingredients in a large pot for thirty minutes. Smash any unbroken grapes with a wooden spoon. Add the cinnamon and cloves. Simmer for ten minutes. Pour into jars and process in boiling water for ten minutes.

(From FoodinJars.com.)

Many ingredients are involved in making the classic taste of tomato ketchup. Though cheap to buy, it's also fun to make and a good gift for friends who put ketchup on everything from eggs to grilled cheese. You'll need a blender, and to cut down on cooking time, you'll want to use a slow cooker. (This is also a good garage sale item to buy.) Start with twelve pounds fresh tomatoes. Peel them using the boiling method discussed earlier. Slice in half and remove the seeds and juice. Seed and slice one pound of combined green and red peppers. Peel and quarter one pound of onions. Blend all of this and then bring to a boil in a large pot. Reduce heat to medium low and simmer for an hour. Add four and a half cups vinegar, four and a half cups sugar, and one-eighth cup canning salt. Continue to simmer until the ketchup thickens. Add the spices: one tablespoon dry mustard, one-half tablespoon red pepper, one-quarter teaspoon allspice, one-half teaspoon cloves, and one-quarter teaspoon cinnamon. You can continue simmering on low over the stove, stirring often, or transfer to a slow cooker for twelve hours. Basically, you want the volume to divide in half until the ketchup is nice and thick. Put the ketchup in twelve half-pint jars, seal, and boil for fifteen minutes. (From PickYourOwn.org.)

CHAPTER SEVEN

PICKLES AND RELISHES

When you hear "pickles," you probably think of cucumbers. Indeed, pickled cucumbers date to ancient times and are probably the best-known pickled item. But actually, most vegetables and fruits can be pickled, along with meats and eggs. Pickling just means preserving in vinegar or salt brine. Common pickled items include green olives, capers, jalapenos, and pepperoncini.

Long before canning was invented, food was pickled to preserve it. Pickled herring (fish) is mentioned in Shakespeare. Early New Orleans settlers preserved all manner of pork (pig jowls, pig tails, pig lips) by pickling, and Creole cooks continue to add flavor to their food with pickled meats. Pickled eggs were a way for farmers in the 1800s to preserve eggs for a month at a time, and you occasionally see jars of pickled eggs at convenience stores or pubs, though they've mostly fallen out of favor.

Which of these are pickles? They all are. A pickle is anything preserved in a salt or vinegar brine. They can be onions *(left)*, eggs *(center)*, or, of course, cucumbers.

When pickling vegetables, you'll probably want to start with the most famous pickle: the dill pickle. Cucumbers are easy to grow, but contrary to popular belief, pickles aren't made with baby cucumbers. Pickling cucumbers are different from slicing cucumbers (which are the big kind you see in the store). Pickling varieties include County Fair, National Pickling, Pickle Bush, Regal, and Saladin. Dill grows like a weed and, in fact, is sometimes called dill weed. Dill pickles call for dill seeds, which grow when the herb flowers and "goes to seed."

Here is how to make dill pickles: Start with three pounds of 4-inch (10 cm) cucumbers. Scrub the vegetables and remove stems, blossoms, and blossom ends. Slice into .25-inch (0.6 cm) rounds. Combine four cups water, four cups white vinegar, one-half cup sugar, and one-third cup pickling salt. Boil until sugar dissolves. Pack cucumber slices into six prepared pint jars. Leave .5 (1.3 cm) inch at the top. Pour the liquid over the cucumbers, still leaving .5 inch (1.3 m) at the top. Seal and boil for ten minutes. Store for a week before eating. (From *Can It!* by Better Homes and Gardens.)

A PLACE FOR PICKLES

In addition to topping sandwiches, pickles can be added to potato salad, salad, soup, and more. You can make a delicious potato chip dip by blending one cup of minced pickles, one tablespoon Worcestershire sauce, and a dash of pickle juice with eight ounces of cream cheese. (From BunsinMyOven.com.) And speaking of sandwiches, pickles taste delicious on peanut butter or grilled cheese.

Pickle juice can be mixed with olive oil to make salad dressing; added to barbeque sauce, tomato juice, and homemade macaroni and cheese for a zesty kick; used as a meat marinade; and used as brine for other vegetables or boiled eggs. You can even use pickle juice to kill weeds, which wither when doused with the vinegar and salt.

Sweet pickles are delicious atop salads and sandwiches, or chopped and added to deviled eggs. To can sweet pickles, slice four pounds pickle cucumbers .5 inch (1.3 cm) thick. In a large bowl, add to the sliced cucumbers one-half cup pickling salt and ice water to cover. Let it sit for twelve hours, adding more ice a few times. Drain and rinse. Prepare five pint jars. Now, in a pot, bring to a boil two minced onions, one-quarter cup minced red pepper, two teaspoons celery salt, one teaspoon dry mustard, one teaspoon pepper, three cups apple cider vinegar, three cups sugar, and three tablespoons pickling spice. Add the cucumbers and return to a boil. Remove from heat, fill the jars, seal, and boil for ten minutes.

As if pickles weren't delicious enough, someone thought of frying them. Fried pickles are a southern delicacy. They are dipped in a batter and fried in oil. You can buy batter mix at the store, but it's also easy to make. Just mix one-half cup flour, one-half teaspoon salt, and any other spices (such as Cajun), with half a cup water. That makes enough batter for two cups of pickle slices. Remove the pickles from the jar, pat them dry, dip them in the batter and fry them in 375-degree F (190 degrees C) oil until golden brown. Remove from the oil with a slotted spoon, and let the pickles drain on paper towels. Dip them in mayonnaise mixed with your homemade ketchup. (Adapted from FoodNetwork.com.)

Pickled peppers are a delicious topping for sandwiches and salads. Start with three pounds of sweet peppers in various colors. Seed and slice. Also slice two large onions. In a large pot, combine four cups sugar, four cups water, three cups white

Pickled peppers add zest to sandwiches. And when you finish eating a jar of pickles, the juice can be used to spice up other recipes.

vinegar, two cups cider vinegar, one tablespoon celery seeds, one tablespoon peppercorns, one teaspoon mustard seeds, four cloves crushed garlic, four bay leaves, and two teaspoons salt. Bring to a boil, stirring. Reduce heat and simmer for twenty minutes. Remove the garlic and bay leaves. Pack the peppers and onions in pint jars, leaving .5 inch (1.3 cm) at the top. Pour the vinegar over the jars, still leaving .5 inch (1.3 cm). Seal and boil the jars for ten minutes. They'll be ready to eat in one week. (From *Can It!* by Better Homes and Gardens.)

ACID A solution that has excess positive hydrogen ions. Sour-tasting liquids like lemon juice and vinegar tend to be acids.

BACTERIA A simple celled organism, some species of which cause sickness.

BLANCHE To steam without fully cooking.

BOTULISM A disease caused by ingesting harmful bacteria growing in spoiled food.

BRINE Salt water used to preserve food.

CANNING Preserving food in jars or cans.

CARBON EMISSIONS Exhaust from cars, homes, or factories that contain carbon dioxide, a greenhouse gas that contributes to global warming.

FERTILIZER Substances, usually high in nitrogen, that make plants grow faster or hardier.

JARRING Preserving food in jars by use of heat and sealing.

PACKING Filling jars with food to be preserved.

PARE To peel.

PASTE TOMATO A tomato used for cooking and canning because of its thick flesh and low juice content.

PECTIN A substance naturally occurring in fruits or purchased in powder or liquid form that is used to thicken jellies and jams.

PICKLE To preserve in an acid, such as vinegar.

PRESERVING Making food last, usually by slowing bacteria growth.

PRESSURE CANNER A pot with a lid, inside which the pressure can be increased, allowing water to boil at higher heat.

PROCESS To boil jars according to instructions in order to preserve the food inside.

SCURVY A disease caused by lack of vitamin C.

URBAN FARM A farm in the city.

WATER BATH CANNING The preserving method in which high acid fruits or vegetables are sealed in jars and boiled (not in a pressure canner).

FOR MORE INFORMATION

Battery Conservancy
One Whitehall Street, 17th Floor
New York, NY 10004
(212) 344-3491
Web site: http://www.thebattery.org
The Battery Conservancy is a public park in Manhattan that
  includes a large urban farm designed to teach young people
  about farming.

City Farmer News
Box 74567, Kitsilano RPO
Vancouver, BC V6K 4P4
Canada
(604) 736-2250
Web site: http://www.cityfarmer.info
City Farmer News features articles about urban farms.

Food Share
90 Croatia Street
Toronto, ON M6H 1K9
Canada
(416) 363-6441
Web site: http:// http://www.foodshare.net
Food Share promotes healthy growing and helps all people
  have access to healthy produce.

4-H
7100 Connecticut Avenue
Chevy Chase, MD 20815
Web site: http://www.4-H.org
4-H is a youth development organization focused on science, citizenship, and healthy living.

4-H Canada
Central Experimental Farm
960 Carling Avenue
Building 26
Ottawa, ON K1A 0C6
Canada
(613) 234-4448
Web site: http://www.4-h-canada.ca
4-H Canada is a youth development organization in Canada.

Future Farmers of America
P.O. Box 68960, 6060 FFA Drive
Indianapolis, IN 46268-0960
(317) 802-6060
Web site: http://www.ffa.org
The Future Farmers of America prepares young people for farming careers.

National Center for Home Food Preservation
The University of Georgia

208 Hoke Smith Annex
Athens, GA 30602-4356
Web site: http://nchfp.uga.edu
The National Center for Home Food Preservation provides information about safely preserving food in the home.

Young Urban Farmer
5863 Leslie Street, Suite 616
Toronto, ON M2H 1J8
Canada
(416) 238-5715
Web site: http://youngurbanfarmers.com
Young Urban Farmers helps people grow food in the city.

WEB SITES

Due to the changing nature of Internet links, Rosen Publishing has developed an online list of Web sites related to the subject of this book. This site is updated regularly. Please use this link to access the list:

http://www.rosenlinks.com/UGFT/Jarr

FOR FURTHER READING

Carle, Meghan, Jill Carle, and Judi Carle. *Teens Cook: How to Cook What You Want to Eat*. New York, NY: Ten Speed, 2004.

Chadwick, Janet. *The Beginner's Guide to Preserving Food at Home: Easy Instructions for Canning, Freezing, Drying, Brining, and Root Cellaring Your Favorite Fruits, Herbs and Vegetables*. North Adams, MA: Storey, 2009.

Costenbader, Carol. *The Big Book of Preserving the Harvest: 150 Recipes for Freezing, Canning, Drying and Pickling Fruits and Vegetables*. North Adams, MA: Storey, 2002.

Crocker, Pat. *Preserving: The Canning and Freezing Guide for All Seasons*. New York, NY: William Morrow, 2012.

Culinary Institute of America. *Preserving*. Hoboken, NJ: Wiley, 2013.

English, Ashleigh. *Homemade Living: Canning & Preserving with Ashley English: All You Need to Know to Make Jams, Jellies, Pickles, Chutneys & More*. New York, NY: Lark, 2010.

Field, Rick, and Rebecca Courchesne. *The Art of Preserving*. San Francisco, CA: Weldon Owen, 2012.

Krissoff, Liana. *Canning for a New Generation: Bold, Fresh Flavors for the Modern Pantry*. New York, NY: Stewart, Tabori & Chang, 2010.

Lawrence, Marie. *The Farmer's Cookbook: A Back to Basics Guide to Making Cheese, Curing Meat, Preserving Produce,*

Baking Bread, Fermenting, and More (Back to Basics Guides). New York, NY: Skyhorse, 2011.

Lewin, Alex. *Real Food Fermentation: Preserving Whole Fresh Food with Live Cultures in Your Home Kitchen*. Minneapolis, MN: Quarry Books, 2012

Megyesi, Jennifer. *The Joy of Keeping a Root Cellar: Canning, Freezing, Drying, Smoking and Preserving the Harvest*. New York, NY: Skyhorse, 2010.

Oster, Ken. *The Complete Guide to Preserving Meat, Fish, and Game: Step-by-Step Instructions to Freezing, Canning, Curing, and Smoking* (Back-to-Basics Cooking). Ocala, FL: Atlantic Publishing, 2011.

Pelzel, Raquel. *Preserving Wild Foods: A Modern Forager's Recipes for Curing, Canning, Smoking, and Pickling*. North Adams, MA: Storey, 2012.

Ruhlman, Michael, Brian Polcyn, and Thomas Keller. *Charcuterie: The Craft of Salting, Smoking, and Curing*. New York, NY: Norton, 2005.

Strawbridge, Dick, and James Strawbridge. *Preserving* (Made at Home). Richmond Hill, Ontario, Canada: Firefly, 2012.

Topp, Ellie, and Margaret Howard. *Preserving Made Easy: Small Batches and Simple Techniques*. Richmond Hill, Ontario, Canada: Firefly, 2012.

Vassallo, Jody, and Clive Bozzard-Hill. *Preserving Basics: 77 Recipes Illustrated Step by Step* (My Cooking Class). Richmond Hill, Ontario, Canada: Firefly, 2012.

Vinton, Sherri Brooks. *Put 'Em Up*. North Adams, MA: Storey, 2010.

Virant, Paul. *The Preservation Kitchen: The Craft of Making and Cooking with Pickles, Preserves, and Aigre-doux*. New York, NY: Ten Speed, 2012.

FICTION:

Horvath, Polly. *The Canning Season*. New York, NY: Square Fish, 2012.

Better Homes and Gardens. *Can It!* Hoboken, NJ: Wiley, 2012.

Campbell, Karly. "Pickle Dip." January 18, 2012. BunsinMyOven
.com. Retrieved March 1, 2013 (http://www.bunsinmyoven
.com/2012/01/18/pickle-dip).

Can & Aerosol News. "The History of Canning." Retrieved
February 2, 2013 (http://www.cannedfood.org/files/library
/pdfs/History-can.pdf).

Center for the Advancement of Health. "Today's Teens Slacking
on Fruit, Veggie Intake." *ScienceDaily*, January 28, 2007.
Retrieved January 23, 2013 (http://www.sciencedaily.com
/releases/2007/01/070128141337.htm).

Couture, Lisa. "The History of Canned Food." April 28, 2010.
Johnson & Wales University Academic Symposium of
Undergraduate Scholarship. Retrieved February 2, 2013
(http://scholarsarchive.jwu.edu/cgi/viewcontent.cgi?article
=1006&context=ac_symposium).

Ferrari, Linda. *Canning & Preserving.* New York, NY: Friedman/
Fairfax, 1994.

Field, Elizabeth. "Marmalade." *New York Times.* Retrieved
February 24, 2013 (http://topics.nytimes.com/top/reference
/timestopics/subjects/m/marmalade/index.html).

Field, Rick, and Rebecca Courchesne. *The Art of Preserving.*
San Francisco, CA: WeldonOwen, 2010.

Food Network. "Almost-Famous Fried Pickles." Retrieved March
1, 2013 (http://www.foodnetwork.com/recipes/food-network
-kitchens/almost-famous-fried-pickles-recipe/index.html).

Fussell, James. "Salsa and Second Chances." *Kansas City Star*, September 20, 2011. Retrieved February 24, 2013 (http://www.dailytidings.com/apps/pbcs.dll/article?AID =/20110920/LIFE/109200304).

Health.gov. "Let the Pyramid Guide Your Food Choices." Retrieved January 23, 2013 (http://www.health.gov /dietaryguidelines/dga2000/document/build.htm).

Kaiser, Emily. "Meyer Lemon Marmalade." *Food & Wine*, December 2007. Retrieved February 24, 2013 (http://www .foodandwine.com/recipes/meyer-lemon-marmalade).

Kendall, P. "Freezing Vegetables." Colorado State University Extension, March 2008. Retrieved March 2, 2013 (http:// www.ext.colostate.edu/pubs/foodnut/09330.html).

Matsumoto, Marc. "Fill Your Kitchen with the Smell of Apple Butter." PBS Food, November 13, 2012. Retrieved February 20, 2013 (http://www.pbs.org/food/fresh-tastes /chunky-apple-butter).

McClellan, Marisa. *Food in Jars: Preserving in Small Batches Year Round*. Philadelphia, PA: Running Press, 2011.

McClellan, Marisa. "Grape Catchup." FoodinJars.com, May 7, 2009. Retrieved February 20, 2013 (http://www.foodinjars .com/2009/05/grape-catchup).

McClellan, Marisa. "Watermelon Jelly Recipe." Foodinjars.com, August 30, 2010. Retrieved February 20, 2013 (http:// www.foodinjars.com/2010/08/watermelon-jelly-recipe).

PickYourOwn.org. "Making and Canning Homemade Natural Ketchup from Fresh Tomatoes Easily." Retrieved March 2, 2013 (http://www.pickyourown.org/ketchupblender.htm).

Terebelski, Dana, and Nancy Ralph. "Pickle History Timeline." New York Food Museum, 2003. Retrieved January 18, 2013 (http://www.nyfoodmuseum.org/_ptime.htm).

TheKitchn.com "What's the Difference Between Jam, Jelly, Conserves, Marmalade, Etc.?" June 25, 2009. Retrieved January 23, 2013 (http://www.thekitchn.com/whats-the -difference-between-j-87558).

University of Wisconsin Extension. "Canning Salsa Safely." 2000. Retrieved March 1, 2013 (http://pepin.uwex.edu /files/2010/10/CanningSalsaSafely.pdf).

U.S. Department of Agriculture. *The Complete Guide to Home Canning and Preserving*. Mineola, NY: Dover, 1999.

Walsh, Danielle. "15 Ways to Use Leftover Pickle Juice." *Bon Appetit*, August 30, 2012. Retrieved March 1, 2013 (http://www.bonappetit.com/blogsandforums/blogs/badaily /2012/08/cook-with-pickle-juice.html).

INDEX

ABOUT THE AUTHOR

Bridget Heos is the author of more than sixty nonfiction books for children and teens. She lives with her husband and four children in Kansas City and has had a garden since grade school.

PHOTO CREDITS

Cover © iStockphoto.com/YinYang; p. 5 imagebroker.net/SuperStock; p. 8 Ann Rosener/Time & Life Pictures/Getty Images; p. 10 Dag Sundberg/Photographer's Choice/Getty Images; p. 12 Elena Dijour/Shutterstock.com; p. 16 Jupiterimages/Brand X Pictures /Thinkstock; p. 18 iStockphoto/Thinkstock; p. 20 Zigzag Mountain Art/Shutterstock.com; p. 23 Andrew Brunk /Shutterstock.com; p. 25 luanateutzi/Shutterstock.com; p. 29 Christian Jung/Shutterstock.com; p. 31 Kevin H. Knuth /Shutterstock.com; p. 35 Helen H. Richardson/Denver Post/ Getty Images; p. 37 Jupiterimages/FoodPix/Getty Images; p. 38 Sally Wallis/Shutterstock.com; p. 41 Fotokostic/Shutterstock.com; p. 43 David P. Smith/Shutterstock; p. 47 Oli Scarff/Getty Images; p. 50 monticello/Shutterstock.com; cover and interior pages (cityscape silhouette) © iStockphoto.com/blackred; cover and interior pages (dirt) © iStockphoto.com/wragg; back cover, interior pages (jar silhouettes) © iStockphoto.com/lumpynoodles; interior pages (silhouette texture) © iStockphoto.com/mon5ter.

Designer: Nicole Russo; Editor: Bethany Bryan;
Photo Researcher: Marty Levick